P9-DFT-501

Contents

Introduction

Wide and varied reading by students is a standard curriculum goal, but book reporting for beginning students? Yes! Book reporting develops the beginning reader's comprehension skills and motivates reluctant readers. Nurturing an early love of reading is an achievement—for both teacher and student—that has its own reward. These teaching suggestions for developing book reporting skills make the task easier.

Assigning book reports gets students to read more often as well as more carefully. Make sure you have plenty of books available. Go out on a limb and use your own public library card if necessary. Take book orders from your students and watch your students' eyes light up when you deliver their special requests.

Read aloud every day. Choose an easy book you'd like to have your students read, or choose a classic. Schedule a silent reading time, daily or weekly, during which everyone reads—even the teacher! (No surreptitious paper grading allowed!)

The linemasters are divided into seven units, with a section of teacher's notes located at the end of each unit. Specific suggestions for the use of each linemaster page will be found in the teacher's notes sections. Although some activities are more appropriate for group use and some for individual use, the teacher's notes suggest how to tailor activities to meet your instructional needs.

Use Unit One to develop systematically a basic book reporting method, then progress as far as your students' reading and writing skills allow. The linemasters in this unit provide a sequential approach to book reporting and should be presented in order. The first eight activities require a minimum of writing. As your students' skills mature, present the rest of the material in this section. The materials may be used as learning centers or class assignments.

Are you tired of, "I liked this book because . . ."? Unit Two provides a dozen alternatives to the traditional written book report. Assign a project from this section anytime you want a change from written book reports.

Units Three, Four, and Five develop appreciation for literary elements: plot development, characterization, and setting, respectively. Expand creative thinking skills and reinforce the comprehension skills taught in your regular reading program with the activities in these units. The activities in each unit are arranged in order of difficulty. Choose the ones that suit your group.

Unit Six introduces your students to reporting about different types of literature. There is a book to suit every taste! The focus is on nonfiction. While students may use nonfiction books for many book reporting activities throughout Units One through Seven, Unit Six activities were designed to encourage reading of nonfiction and to help students adapt the basic book reporting strategy to nonfiction. Use the materials in this unit at any time.

Use Unit Seven to help your students develop a sense of accomplishment. You may wish to start your book reporting program with one of these reading motivators. Most of these motivators can be used for the individual student or as a display for class competition.

Watch your students become avid readers, eager to do more than just show and tell about the books they've read!

UNIT ONE

Tell All About It!

GETTING READY

It is fun to tell your friends about stories you have enjoyed.

1. Put an **X** beside the things you would tell a friend about your favorite cartoon show.

   a. ____ the name of the show

   b. ____ who is in the show

   c. ____ what your mother was doing that day

   d. ____ the exciting parts

   e. ____ what you had to eat after the show

   f. ____ why you liked it

2. Fill in these facts about your favorite cartoon show.

   a. The title is _____

   b. Some of the people and animals in the story are _____

   _____

   c. The most important person or animal is _____

   d. Tell about the most exciting part. _____

   _____

   _____

Draw a picture on the back about another exciting part.

OFF TO A GOOD START

When you tell about a story, remember to give the title.
Always use a capital letter to begin the first word in a title.
Use capital letters to begin all the other important words, too.

1. Circle the capital letters in these titles.

   a. If I Ran the Zoo

   b. The Wind in the Willows

   c. Horton Hatches the Egg

   d. Little House in the Big Woods

   e. Green Eggs and Ham

Use capitals to begin words such as these when they are the first word in a title:

and of in the for by a to an

But do not use capitals for these words when they are in the middle of a title.

2. Circle the letters in these titles that should be capitalized.

   a. snow white and the seven dwarfs

   b. cricket in a thicket

   c. the selfish giant

PUT ON THE CAPS!

Read these rules for writing titles:
- Capitalize the first letter of the first word.
- Capitalize the first letter of all other important words.
- Do NOT capitalize words such as these when you use them in the middle of a title:

and   by   of   for   to   the   a   an

1. Rewrite each title, putting in the capital letters.

   a. john and henry see a parade

   _____

   b. if i ran the zoo

   _____

   c. the little red hen

   _____

   d. popeye and friends

   _____

   e. how to build a treehouse

   _____

2. Write the titles of two books or TV shows. Put on the caps!

   a. _____

   b. _____

WHO DID IT?

When you tell about a book, you should give the title and the name of the person who wrote the story. A person who writes books or stories is an author.

1. Circle the author of each book.

   Example: *The Cat in the Hat* by (Dr. Seuss)

   a. *Puff The Magic Dragon* by Romeo Muller

   b. *Freckle Juice* by Judy Blume

   c. *Eddie's Happenings* by Carolyn Haywood

   d. *The Tale of Peter Rabbit* by Beatrix Potter

Pictures make a story more interesting. The person who draws the pictures is an illustrator.

2. Circle the name of the illustrator.

   a. *Warton and Morton* by Russell E. Erickson, pictures by Lawrence di Fiori

   b. *Give a Magic Show!* by Burton and Rita Marks, illustrated by Don Madden

   c. *Three by the Sea* by Edward Marshall, pictures by James Marshall

FOLLOW THE FACT-FINDERS

When you tell about a story, follow these six fact-finding questions.

1. What is the title?

2. Who is the author?

3. Who is in the story?

4. When does the story happen?

5. Where does the story happen?

6. What is one of the most exciting things that happens?

Match each picture below with one of the fact-finding questions. Write the number of the question in the corner of the picture that answers the question.

Beginning Book Reporting reproducible page, copyright © 1984 Pitman Learning, Inc.

CAN YOU REMEMBER?

Match each of the six fact-finding questions with a picture. Draw lines.

When does the story happen?

Where does the story happen?

Who is in the story?

What is the title?

Who is the author?

What is one of the most exciting things that happens?

Name _____

USE THE SIX FACT-FINDERS

Complete the six facts for a book you have enjoyed.

1. What is the title? _____

2. Who is the author? _____

3. Who is in the story? _____

_____

4. When does the story happen? _____

_____

5. Where does the story happen? _____

_____

6. What are the most exciting things that happen? _____

_____

_____

_____

_____

Draw a picture on the back about an exciting part.

I LIKE TV TOO!

Use some of the fact-finders to tell about a TV show you like.

1. What is the title? _____

_____

2. Who is in the story? _____

_____

_____

3. When does the story happen? _____

_____

_____

4. Where does the story happen? _____

_____

_____

5. What are the most exciting things that happen? _____

_____

_____

_____

_____

Draw a picture on the back about an exciting part.

Name _____

SENTENCES MAKE SENSE

On a piece of paper, write the facts for a book you have enjoyed. Use your facts to fill in these sentences.

1. The book I read was _____ .

2. It was written by _____ .

3. The main characters in the story are _____

_____ .

4. The characters lived during the time _____

_____ .

5. The story takes place in _____

_____ .

Write your own sentences to tell about the most exciting things that happen in the story. _____

_____

_____

_____

On the back, draw a picture of an exciting scene from the story.

Name _____

BOOK REPORT FORM:
SENTENCES

On another piece of paper, write the facts for a book you have enjoyed. Tell about these things:

- title
- author
- main characters
- time
- place
- exciting events

Use the facts to write your own sentences about this book.

1. _____

   _____

2. _____

   _____

3. _____

   _____

4. _____

   _____

5. _____

   _____

6. _____

   _____

BOOK REPORT FORM: PARAGRAPHS

On another piece of paper, write the facts for a book you have enjoyed. Tell about these things:

- title
- author
- main characters
- time
- place
- exciting events

Now use the facts to write two paragraphs about this book. In the first paragraph, tell the title, author, characters, time, and place for this book. Be sure to write complete sentences. On the back of this page, write the second paragraph, telling about the exciting parts of the story.

_____

_____

_____

_____

_____

_____

_____

_____

_____

TEACHER'S NOTES

The activities in this unit are designed to develop a basic book reporting strategy. Use them in the order presented, skipping the activities you think are not needed for your group.

GETTING READY
page 4

Objective: The student will apply book reporting skills to a favorite cartoon show.

Suggestions for Use: Stimulate interest by asking your students to name their favorite cartoon shows. Then ask if they have seen a show they wanted to tell someone else about. Have the students complete the worksheet. Encourage them to tell only the facts of the story when reporting. Then discuss the responses with them.

Answer Key: 1. a, b, d, f

OFF TO A GOOD START
page 5

Objective: The student will become aware of the importance of reporting a title and of a correct form for writing titles.

Suggestions for Use: Review the term "capital (upper-case) letters" if needed. Explain that important words in a title convey key information. Discuss answers after Part 2 is completed.

Answer Key: 2a. Snow White and the Seven Dwarfs
b. Cricket in a Thicket
c. The Selfish Giant

PUT ON THE CAPS!
page 6

Objective: The student will use capital letters correctly when writing titles.

Suggestions for Use: Review the rules for capitalizing words in titles as presented on the worksheet. On the board, write some titles of stories the group has enjoyed. When the students have completed the worksheets, conduct class discussion to share the last section.

Answer Key: 1a. John and Henry See a Parade   b. If I Ran the Zoo
c. The Little Red Hen   d. Popeye and Friends   e. How to Build a Treehouse

WHO DID IT?
page 7

Objective: The student will identify credits for authors and illustrators within the given titles.

Suggestions for Use: Introduce the terms "author," "illustrator," "pictures by," and "illustrated by" before the students complete the worksheets. If appropriate for the level of your group, follow up this activity with a discussion of favorite authors.

FOLLOW THE FACT-FINDERS
page 8

Objective: The student will become familiar with a basic book reporting method.

Suggestions for Use: Read aloud a book that is a favorite for your students' age group. Then introduce and answer the six fact-finders for that story. Use this worksheet as a review. In your follow-up discussion, show how the answers to each of the fact-finder questions helps to retell a story.

Answer Key:

CAN YOU REMEMBER?
page 9

Objective: The student will recall the meanings of each of the six fact-finding questions.

Suggestions for Use: Use this worksheet as a review of the six fact-finding questions. For an additional activity, have your students cut out the pictures and paste them in an order that shows the basic book report sequence: title, author, characters, time, place, and events.

Answer Key:

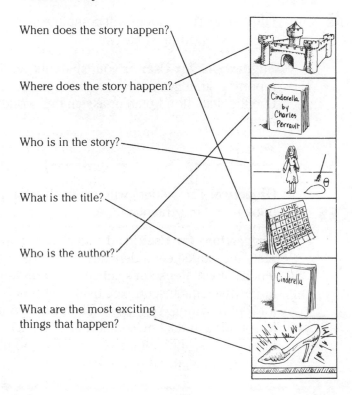

When does the story happen?

Where does the story happen?

Who is in the story?

What is the title?

Who is the author?

What are the most exciting things that happen?

USE THE SIX FACT-FINDERS
page 10

Objective: The student will use the basic book reporting strategy for a book he or she has enjoyed.

Suggestions for Use: Choose a read-aloud book. Introduce the term "character." Have your students complete the worksheet independently after you read the story. Use this form whenever it suits your instructional needs. If the maturity level of your group is high, make this an independent assignment.

I LIKE TV TOO!
page 11

Objective: The student will use the book reporting strategy to tell about a favorite TV show.

Suggestions for Use: This worksheet is designed as a home assignment. Decide on the type of TV program you want your students to watch. The students will enjoy sharing their reports.

SENTENCES MAKE SENSE
page 12

Objective: The student will complete sentences as he or she follows the book reporting strategy.

Suggestions for Use: As your students' abilities to use the book reporting strategy mature, combining sentences is the next logical step. Use the read-aloud plan or assign this worksheet as an independent activity.

BOOK REPORT FORM: SENTENCES
page 13

Objective: The student will use the book reporting strategy to write a book report in sentence form.

Suggestions for Use: Read a story aloud and have your students complete the worksheet independently. Have the students read their sentences aloud. Reuse this activity as an independent worksheet. Taking notes in a logical sequence before writing is an important technique for report writing. You may wish to have your students bring their notes to you for a quick check before they write the sentences. Explain the term "events." Encourage your students to use the sentence-combining technique suggested previously.

BOOK REPORT FORM: PARAGRAPHS
page 14

Objective: The student will use the book reporting strategy to write a book report in paragraph form.

Suggestions for Use: Having a set of notes in logical sequence will make the transition to paragraph writing easier. First, you may wish to do this activity with the entire class from a read-aloud book. Use this worksheet as often as you wish.

UNIT TWO

Book Report Projects

Name _____

COMIC STRIP STORY

Make ___ ___ ic strip about a book you have enjoyed.

1. In Box A ___ ___ the title and the author.

2. In Box B, intr ___ the characters.

3. In Box C, show the where and when.

4. In the remaining boxes, show the exciting events. Use cartoon speech balloons if the characters speak. If you need more boxes, use another sheet of paper. Draw the extra boxes to match the ones on this paper.

A	B	C

Name _____

BOOKMOBILE MOBILES

You will need:
- a favorite book
- a coat hanger
- scissors
- heavy paper
- hole punch
- crayons
- yarn or string (7 pieces, different lengths)

To make the mobile:

1. Using the pattern, cut seven bookmobiles from heavy paper. Punch a hole at the top of each one.

2. Write your name on both sides of one bookmobile. For the other six, write one fact about your book on both sides of the bookmobile. These are the facts:
   - title
   - author
   - main characters
   - time
   - place
   - one main event

3. Draw designs around the writing on the bookmobiles.

4. Thread each piece of yarn or string through a hole and knot it. Tie the other end of each piece of yarn or string to the hanger. Spread the pieces out for balance. Hang the mobile from its hook end.

BOOKMOBILE PATTERN

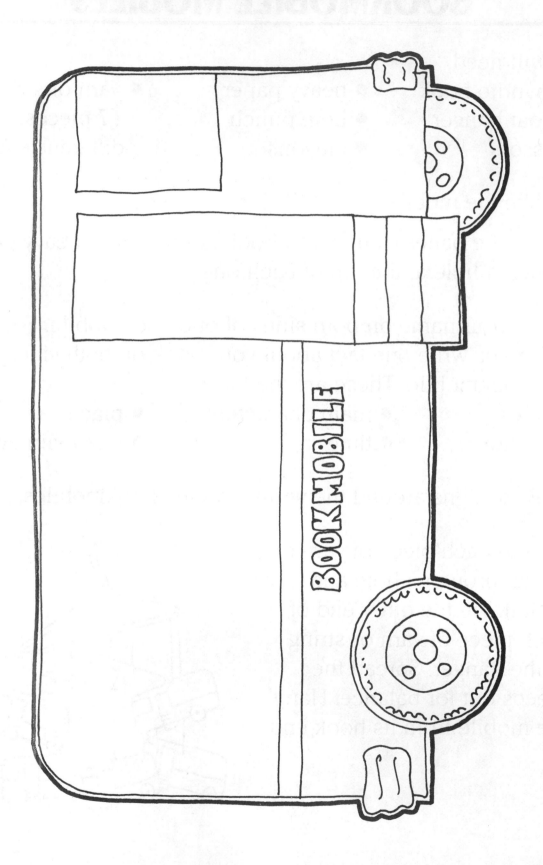

BOOKMOBILE

Name _____

DRESS-UP TIME

Join the Book Parade by dressing up like your favorite book character!

1. First, on another piece of paper write the facts about this book:
   - title
   - author
   - favorite character
   - where
   - when
   - exciting events

2. Plan your costume.
   a. You could make a costume from a large piece of butcher paper or brown wrapping paper. Lie down on the paper, and have a friend draw the outline of your body. Color the front of the costume. Cut out the costume along the outline. Tape the costume to your shoulders.

   b. Instead, you may wish to make a grocery bag mask. Pull the bag over your head, covering your face. Feel your eyes, nose, and mouth through the bag. Carefully mark their placement. Take off the bag. Cut holes for your eyes, nose, and mouth. Decorate the bag.

   c. Will you need any props? If your character is a baseball player, the props you might use are a baseball glove, a ball, and perhaps a bat.

3. Practice telling the facts about your book. On Book Parade Day be ready to tell them to the class.

BOOK BANNER

Make a book banner for a book you enjoyed.

Materials
- a book you have read!
- scissors
- glue
- a piece of white paper
- crayons or felt-tipped markers
- banner pattern—Parts 1 and 2

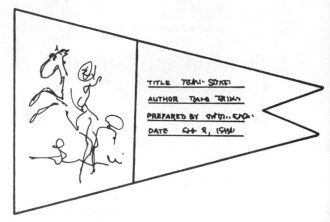

Directions

1. Plan your banner. Look at the banner pattern. Find the place for a picture about your book. Find the lines for writing the title, the author's name, and your name.

2. Plan your picture. Choose an interesting event from the story. Draw your picture on the piece of white paper. Make sure your picture will fit in the space on the banner.

3. Cut out the banner. Glue the two parts together. While you wait for the glue to dry, complete the next step.

4. Use a dark-colored crayon or marker to print the title, the author, and your name on the banner.

5. Trim your picture to fit on the banner and then glue it in place. Hang up your book banner!

BOOK BANNER PATTERN—PART 1

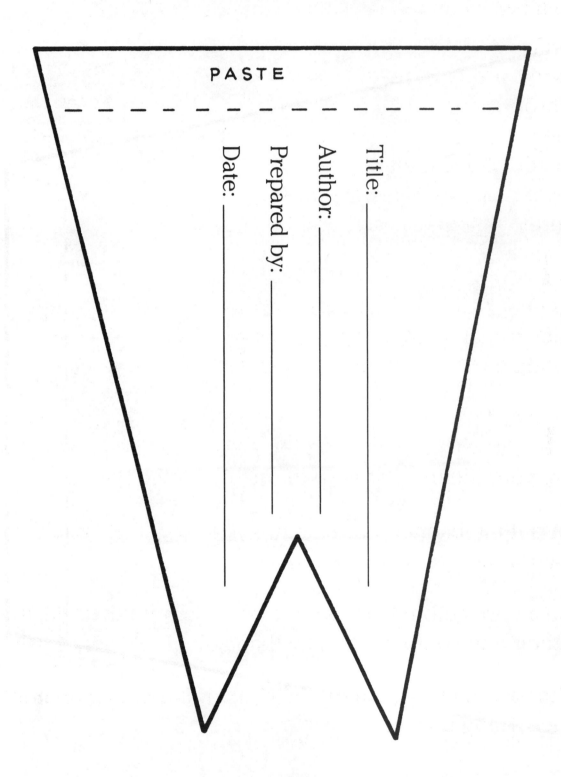

PASTE

Title:

Author:

Prepared by:

Date:

BOOK BANNER PATTERN—PART 2

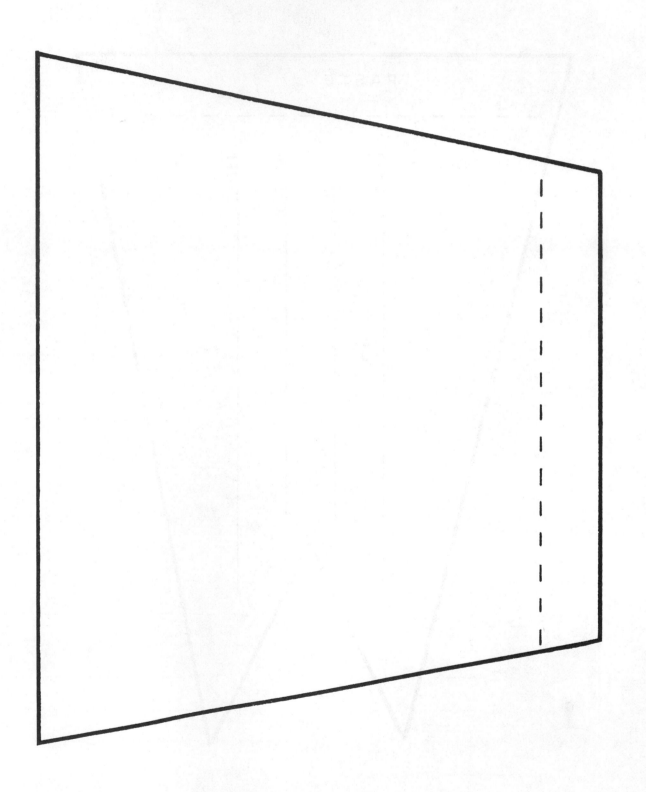

Name _____

TELLTALE TITLE

Write the title and author of your book on the lines below.

Title: _____

Author: _____

Write the title of your book in the boxes below. Put one letter in each box. Now use the title to tell a tale about your book. Use each letter in the title as the beginning of a word, phrase, or sentence about the book. If your title is very long, do as many as you can.

Name _____

MAKE A MAP

Make a map to tell about a book you enjoyed. The map should show where the main events happened and where the characters lived. Label the places you put on your map. You may also want to draw pictures of the main events.

You will need:

- a book you have enjoyed
- scratch paper
- large sheet of white paper
- crayons, markers, or colored pencils

Directions

1. Make a rough plan of your map on scrap paper.

2. Give your map a title.

3. Have your teacher check your plan.

4. Now draw your map on good paper. Print the names of the places neatly, then color your map.

5. At the bottom, print the following:

   This map was designed for _____
   (write the title of the book)

   by _____ (write your name).

6. Hang up your map!

THOSE CHARACTERS!

A bad character may cause problems for the story's hero or heroine. Fill in the facts for a story that has a bad character.

1. Title: _____

2. Author: _____

3. The hero or heroine: _____

   The bad character: _____

4. When: _____

5. Where: _____

6. Tell the problems that the bad character caused for the hero or heroine. Tell how the person solved these

   problems. _____

   _____

   _____

7. Tell how you would have solved the problems the heroine

   or hero faced. _____

   _____

   _____

   _____

STICK PUPPETS: THE SCRIPT

Make stick puppets to present a scene from a book you have enjoyed. First, give these facts of the chosen scene.

1. Title: _____

2. Author: _____

3. Characters in the scene: _____

_____

4. Events of this scene: _____

_____

_____

Write the script on the next page. Here is the form to use for a script to show how the characters talk to each other.

Snow White: Oh, Doc! Sneezy has been sneezing so much he can't even eat!

Sneezy: Ah—chooooo! Ahchooo! Ah-chooo!

Doc: Put the cat outside. That will help.

Snow White: Why didn't I think of that?

Sneezy: I feel better already.

Beginning Book Reporting reproducible page, copyright © 1984 Pitman Learning, Inc.

STICK PUPPETS: WRITING THE SCRIPT

First, write the name of the character who is speaking. Then write what that character says.

_____ : _____

_____

_____ : _____

_____

_____ : _____

_____

_____ : _____

_____

_____ : _____

_____

_____ : _____

_____

MAKING STICK PUPPETS

Now make the puppets. You will need a puppet for each character in your script.

Materials
- popsicle sticks
- white construction paper
- stage (a desk covered with a tablecloth will do)
- crayons or felt-tipped pens
- glue
- scissors

Directions
1. Draw the character on construction paper. Make the largest character about 10 inches tall.

2. Cut out the character, then use it as a pattern to trace and cut out the back of the character.

3. Color the character front and back.

4. Glue the stick between the front and back pieces of the character. Leave part of the stick hanging from the bottom to use as a handle.

5. Allow the glue to dry.

6. Practice reading the script and using the stick puppets on stage.

7. Be ready to perform on Puppet Show Day!

Name _____

PACK YOUR TRUNK FOR . . .

Imagine that you have been invited to visit your favorite book character! Complete these plans for your trip.

1. Character's name: _____

2. Title: _____

3. Author: _____

4. Where will you go? _____

5. How will you travel? _____

6. What clothes and other things will you need to pack? _____

_____

_____

7. Write one question you will ask your character when you

arrive. _____

_____

8. Tell one thing you and your character will do while you

visit. _____

_____

_____

GRAB BAG

This is a guessing game to try with your group.

1. You will need:

   a. A story you and your friends have enjoyed reading.

   b. A grocery bag.

   c. Clues about your story to put in the bag. Some suggestions are pictures of toys or objects neatly cut from magazines. If you can't find a picture, draw one!

2. Before game time:

   a. Write the title and author of the story on a piece of paper. Give it to your teacher.

   b. Put the clues in the grocery bag before you bring them to school.

3. To play the game:

   a. Take one thing out of your bag.

   b. Ask someone to tell you what it is.

   c. Ask if anyone knows the title of the book.

   d. Repeat these steps until someone guesses your title.

   e. After someone guesses your title, take the rest of the clues out of your bag, one by one, and tell why you chose each one.

Name _____

TALK SHOW INTERVIEW

Pretend you are a talk show host or hostess, and your favorite character is a guest on your show.

1. Complete these facts about the book and the character:

   a. Character's name: _____

   b. Title: _____

   c. Author: _____

   d. One subject your character would like to talk about:

   _____

2. Now write the interview on another piece of paper. Follow these directions.

   a. Write a title for your talk show.

   b. Prepare the script. Write at least three questions you would ask your guest, and give the guest's replies. Use this form:

   Your name: Hello, Mother Goose. How are your children?

   Mother Goose: They are fine, except for Bo-Peep. She can never find her sheep! I'm so upset!

3. When you are finished, you and a friend may like to present your talk show to your class. Be sure to practice reading smoothly and with expression.

TEACHER'S NOTES

B ook reports do not need to be written to indicate what a student has gleaned from a book. When you and your students are in the book report doldrums, try one of the projects in this unit. Many groups will benefit from using these highly motivating escapes from traditional book report forms. Follow the fact-finding strategy when appropriate.

COMIC STRIP STORY
page 20

Objective: The student will use the book reporting strategy to draw a comic strip for a book read independently.

Suggestions for Use: After the comic strips have been drawn, you may wish to cut off the directions and display the book report comics. You may also bind these reports into a class comic book. Use tagboard for the cover and brads to hold the pages together.

BOOKMOBILE MOBILES
pages 21–22

Objective: The student will construct a book mobile as a summary of a book read independently.

Suggestions for Use: Brighten up your winter classroom by having your students make book mobiles. Have the students bring in the needed supplies in advance so everyone will be ready on construction day. Remind the students to write the information on both sides of their bookmobiles. The designs or drawings they add should help to tell about their books. Display the completed book mobiles across the classroom on strong cord.

DRESS-UP TIME
page 23

Objective: The student will participate in a Book Parade by dressing up as a favorite book character.

Suggestions for Use: Decide first how elaborate you want to make the Book Parade and if you wish to include other groups. Organize the students in groups of two or three, and set up practice times for the informal oral book reporting. If Halloween activities are discouraged in your school, a Book Parade would make a great substitute! This activity is also suitable for the end of the school year.

BOOK BANNER
pages 24-26

Objective: The student will make a book banner to advertise a book read independently.

Suggestions for Use: Book Banners are appropriate at any time as a follow-up to independent reading or as an adjunct to written book reports. Following the given patterns, you may wish to make larger patterns by using an overhead projector, or you may wish to make banner patterns of your own design.

TELLTALE TITLE
page 27

Objective: The student will demonstrate comprehension of an independently read book by using the title as a guide to writing about the book.

Suggestions for Use: You may wish to introduce *Telltale Title* as an activity for a story from a reader. Encourage your students to choose short titles. A completed *Telltale Title* would look like the following:

Played in Mr. McGregor's garden
Enjoyed eating the carrots
The owner got angry
Enjoyed eating the cabbages
Ran as fast as he could

Raced away from Mr. McGregor
Admitted his mistake to his mother
Battled with Mr. McGregor
Boldly ate the lettuce
It was frightening to hide in the
   sprinkling can
There was danger for Peter in
   Mr. McGregor's garden

MAKE A MAP
page 28

Objective: The student will plan a map to show the locale and events of a book read independently.

Suggestions for Use: This project will delight even your most reluctant readers and challenge their creative instincts. The story could also be from a reader instead of from a book read independently. Encourage your students to use their imaginations as well as their reading comprehension skills. Display the completed maps.

THOSE CHARACTERS!
page 29

Objective: The student will identify the anti-hero element in plot development.

Suggestions for Use: Use this activity for any story with an obvious antagonist. Introduce different types of antagonists, such as monsters or evil imaginary creatures. Then give examples of obvious human antagonists—people whose evil characteristics are obstacles to the hero of the story. The queen in "Snow White" or Captain Hook in *Peter Pan* are two examples of such antagonists. Then, if your group needs a challenge, introduce the term "antagonist." Give examples of antagonists who are not necessarily "villains." Explain how an antagonist can be the hero's opponent or obstacle without being a truly "bad" person.

STICK PUPPETS
pages 30–32

Objective: The student will make stick puppets and dramatize a scene from a favorite book.

Suggestions for Use: This activity has four phases. The student reads a book and chooses a scene to dramatize. A script is written, and the puppets are made. Able students may carry out the activity independently, or you may wish to assign a group of students to work on this project for a common favorite book.

PACK YOUR TRUNK FOR . . .
page 33

Objective: The student will plan an imaginary trip to visit a favorite book character.

Suggestions for Use: This worksheet is designed to be used as an independent activity after a book has been enjoyed. The divergent thinking required should challenge even the most creative students in your class. If the majority of your students is familiar with the books, you could play this group game: Read aloud one of the completed papers, omitting line one. As the plans for the trip are revealed, have the rest of the group guess the character.

GRAB BAG
page 34

Objective: The student will demonstrate an understanding of an independently read book by choosing appropriate clues to the story.

Suggestions for Use: Play this game with a small or large group. The students will need to be familiar with most of the books. You may wish to assign each student a book title in secret from a list of the group's favorites. You can change *Grab Bag* to an oral book reporting strategy by eliminating the guessing game aspect and having the student explain how each item or picture fits the story.

TALK SHOW INTERVIEW
page 35

Objective: The student will demonstrate understanding of a book character by writing an imaginary talk show interview with that character.

Suggestions for Use: Your students will enjoy writing an imaginary interview with a favorite character. Explain that key events in the plot could be used as interview questions. After the interview has been written, a classmate could act as the favorite character, and the interview could be presented as a skit.

UNIT THREE

Understanding Plot Development

Name _____

FINDING THE STORY PROBLEM

Complete the following for a story you have read and enjoyed.

1. Title: _____

2. Author: _____

3. Main characters: _____

_____

4. What problem did the main characters have to solve? ____

_____

_____

_____

5. How did the main characters solve this problem? _____

_____

_____

_____

_____

Draw a picture on the back that will show the story problem.

Beginning Book Reporting reproducible page, copyright © 1984 Pitman Learning, Inc.

MORE STORY PROBLEMS

Complete the following for a book or story you have read.

1. Title: _____

2. Author: _____

3. Main characters: _____

_____

4. Tell what problem the main characters had to solve: _____

_____

_____

_____

5. Tell how the main characters solved the problem. _____

_____

_____

_____

6. Sometimes a story has more than one problem that the characters have to solve. Did this story have more than one? _____ If so, tell about it. _____

_____

_____

Name _____

SOLVING THE PROBLEM

Complete the following for a book you have read.

1. Title: _____

2. Author: _____

3. Main characters: _____

_____

4. The problem that the characters had to solve in this book was _____

_____

_____

5. How did the characters solve the problem? _____

_____

_____

_____

6. Think of another way the characters could have solved their problem, and then write about it. _____

_____

_____

_____

Name _____

PROBLEM TYPES

Complete the following for a book you have read.

1. Title: _____

2. Author: _____

3. Main characters: _____

_____

4. The main problem in this story was _____

_____

_____

5. Did this story have a second problem? ____ If so, tell about

   it. _____

_____

_____

6. Think about the main problem. Put an **X** beside the phrase
   that best tells the cause of the problem.

   ____ the character's own personality

   ____ another person or group of people

   ____ an animal, the weather, or something magical

Name _____

DRAW THE MAIN EVENTS

Complete the following for a story you enjoyed.

1. Title: _____

2. Author: _____

3. Characters: _____

_____

4. Now tell the important parts of this story, in order, by drawing a picture in each box. Put captions on your pictures if you wish to. If you need more boxes, draw them on the back of this paper.

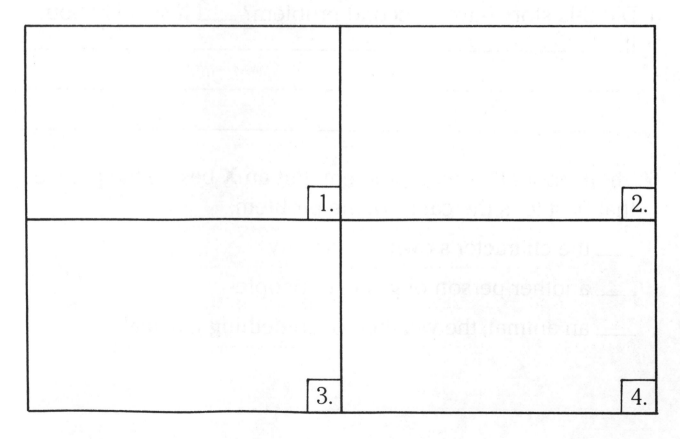

Beginning Book Reporting reproducible page, copyright © 1984 Pitman Learning, Inc.

Name _____

TELL THE MAIN EVENTS

Complete the following for a story you enjoyed.

1. Title: _____

2. Author: _____

3. Characters: _____

_____

Now tell the main events in this story. Use the characters' names instead of "he" or "she." Ask yourself, "What are the most important steps in this story?"

1. _____

2. _____

3. _____

4. _____

5. _____

6. _____

7. _____

8. _____

9. _____

10. _____

FINDING THE CLIMAX

Complete the following.

1. Title: _____

2. Author: _____

3. Characters: _____

_____

The climax is the most exciting part of a story. It is usually near the end of the story.

4. What problem did the characters have to solve? _____

_____

_____

5. How did the characters begin to solve the problem? _____

_____

_____

6. Tell what happened in the most exciting part of the story.

_____

_____

_____

WRITE A NEW ENDING

After the climax, a story usually ends quickly. It is fun to imagine new endings to stories.

1. Remember the main events in "Jack and the Beanstalk." Jack is the main character. His problem is that he must take the golden goose and escape from the giant. He cuts down the beanstalk and kills the giant. Jack and his mother then live happily ever after.

2. Imagine that when Jack cuts down the beanstalk, the giant doesn't die. What could happen next? Use your idea to write a new ending. _____

_____

_____

_____

_____

_____

_____

_____

Name _____

A NEW STORY ENDING

Think of a story you have enjoyed. Complete the following for that story.

1. Title: _____

2. Author: _____

3. Characters: _____

_____

4. What problem needed to be solved? _____

_____

_____

5. What was the story's climax? _____

_____

6. Tell another way the problem could have been solved. Use your idea to write a new ending. Use the back of the paper if you need more room. Let your imagination go! _____

_____

_____

_____

_____

Beginning Book Reporting reproducible page, copyright © 1984 Pitman Learning, Inc.

CLIMBING THE STORY STEP MOUNTAIN

Following the parts of a story is like climbing up and down a mountain.

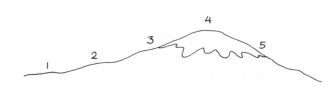

1. characters and setting

2. the main problem

3. a second problem

4. the climax

5. the main problem's solution

These sentences are from the story of Hansel and Gretel. **Number** the parts to show the correct order. The numbers will **match** the story steps shown on the mountain above.

_____ The witch was going to cook and eat Hansel. But Gretel pushed the witch into the fire!

_____ Hansel and Gretel lived in the forest with their parents.

_____ Now the witch was dead. Hansel and Gretel found jewels and money at the witch's house. They took them home to their parents. Now they would not be poor anymore.

_____ The family was very poor and had little food.

_____ The children got lost. They found a gingerbread house to eat, but an old witch lived there.

PICTURE THE PLOT

Follow the story steps for a book you have enjoyed. Write one or two sentences for each step. (You will not be retelling the whole story.) Use the story step mountain as a reminder.

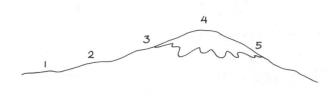

1. characters and setting

2. the main problem

3. a second problem

4. the climax

5. the main problem's solution

1. _____

_____

2. _____

_____

3. _____

_____

4. _____

_____

5. _____

_____

TEACHER'S NOTES

All readers will benefit from an appreciation and understanding of plot development. The basic elements of plot can be applied to stories in readers, to television shows, to skits and plays, and, of course, to books. This unit helps develop an understanding of the basic elements of plot design. It is organized to help you teach those elements in an order that reflects plot development. The illustration on the *Picture the Plot* worksheet presents the classic plot peak, which this unit mirrors.

The activities requiring the student to write new endings provide opportunities for divergent (creative) thinking. Everyone in your group will benefit from this challenge, and some responses will surprise you!

FINDING THE STORY PROBLEM
page 42

Objective: The student will identify the central conflict for a story.

Suggestions for Use: Use this activity for any story your students have read independently or for one you have read aloud to them. Use this page several times during the year.

MORE STORY PROBLEMS
page 43

Objective: The student will identify the central conflict for a given story and any complications that add to the story problem.

Suggestions for Use: Use this worksheet as a directed activity for a first exposure, then reuse it as an independent activity. It can be used several times during the year.

SOLVING THE PROBLEM
page 44

Objective: The student will identify the central conflict and its resolution and will propose another way to solve the problem.

Suggestions for Use: Use this worksheet for a story that the entire group has enjoyed. Have a brainstorming session with the group to think of other ways the problem could have been solved. Follow these brainstorm session guidelines: (1) stick to the subject and (2) anything on the topic is acceptable—no judgments are allowed. After you declare the brainstorming session over, you can have the group review the list for practicality and acceptability. During the year, reuse this worksheet, with or without the brainstorming session, to refine problem identification and solving skills.

PROBLEM TYPES
page 45

Objective: The student will identify the central conflict and will recognize the type of conflict for a given story.

Suggestions for Use: Use this worksheet as a directed activity for a first exposure, then reuse as an independent activity. It can be used several times during the year.

DRAW THE MAIN EVENTS
page 46

Objective: The student will identify the main events of a given story.

Suggestions for Use: There will always be a student who loves to relate every detail of a story! Encourage students to stick closely to the important facts relating to the story problem, its complications, the solution to the problem, and the ending of the story. Use this activity or the following one many times during the year. The ability to identify main events will produce better note-taking and report-writing skills as well as clearer thinking.

TELL THE MAIN EVENTS
page 47

Objective: The student will list the main events for a given story.

Suggestions for Use: Encourage students to use specific nouns and short sentences or phrases. You may wish to introduce this activity by using a story that the group has read from a reader. Then have students attempt to list main events for an entire book read independently.

FINDING THE CLIMAX
page 48

Objective: The student will identify the climax of a given story.

Suggestions for Use: Use this worksheet for a group activity and accompany it with a discussion of plot development. Have the students, as a group, identify the climaxes of other stories they have enjoyed. You can also have the students suggest other ways the story problem could have been solved.

WRITE A NEW ENDING
page 49

Objective: The student will write a new ending for a familiar story.

Suggestions for Use: The students may present their new endings orally or in writing. Your students will benefit from the divergent thinking this worksheet requires. Have the students illustrate the new endings. Make a class book or display of their work.

A NEW STORY ENDING
page 50

Objective: The student will write a new ending for a book read independently.

Suggestions for Use: Use this page as an alternative to the fact-finding report form. Have the students illustrate the new ending. Remember that your acceptance and enjoyment of their creative endeavors is a main ingredient in the development of divergent thinking.

CLIMBING THE STORY STEP MOUNTAIN
page 51

Objective: The student will identify plot structure elements reflected through a familiar fairy tale.

Suggestions for Use: Use this as an independent worksheet. As a sequencing activity, it will help show that plot structure elements are quite natural and can sometimes be identified easily even by children. You may wish to discuss the elements of plot before or after your students complete the exercise. Point out that at step 1, the author gives the background of the story, telling about the characters and the setting. At step 2, the story is developed, and the main problem is shown. Step 3 reveals a second problem (or "complication" of the main problem). The climax (step 4) is an event that usually is followed by a solution (step 5) to the main problem.

Answer Key: 4, 1, 5, 2, 3

PICTURE THE PLOT
page 52

Objective: The student will use plot structure elements in retelling stories.

Suggestions for Use: Your students do not need to master the names of the plot structure elements. Help them to understand and identify these elements as stories unfold. Begin with a clear-cut example and identify the elements as you or the students read the story. Then complete the worksheet as a group activity. Reuse this activity as the year progresses. You could also have the students draw and complete their own plot structure mountains. Or conduct a class project of a *Story Step Mountain* mural, illustrating a story that everyone knows. You may also wish to use the *Picture the Plot* page as an independent activity to challenge more capable students.

UNIT FOUR

Appreciating Story Characters

IMPORTANT CHARACTERS

A character is a person, animal, or other creature in a story. The most important male character in a story is the hero. The most important female character is the heroine.

1. Name two TV show heroines or heroes that are people.

   a. _____ b. _____

2. Name two TV show heroes or heroines that are not people.

   a. _____ b. _____

3. Name two heroines or heroes from books you have enjoyed.

   a. _____ b. _____

4. Heroes and heroines are special because they usually have good qualities we admire. Circle the qualities they probably would show. A hero or heroine might be:

   kind   brave   quick-thinking   stingy   honest
   rude   thoughtful   careless   beautiful   strong

5. Which story character do you most admire? _____

   _____

6. Why do you admire this character? _____

   _____

   _____

MORE THAN SKIN DEEP

Choose a character from a story or book you enjoyed reading. Think about the words the author uses to tell you about this character. The author should tell you how the character looks and how the character acts, thinks, and feels. Complete the following facts about this character and the story.

1. Character's name: _____

2. Title and author: _____

   _____

3. List words or phrases the author uses to tell you what the character looks like.

   _____ _____ _____

   _____ _____ _____

4. Now list words or phrases that tell about the character's personality—how the character acts, thinks, and feels.

   _____ _____ _____

   _____ _____ _____

5. Does this character act the way you think he or she should act? Explain your answer. _____

   _____

   _____

DESCRIBE A CHARACTER

An author usually will tell you how a character looks and will give you ideas about the character's personality.

1. Read each sentence below. Write **L** if the sentence tells how the character looks. Write **P** if the sentence tells about the character's personality.

   ____ a. Ted is friendly.   ____ d. Dr. Hall wears a
                                            white uniform.
   ____ b. Sue loves jokes.
                                    ____ e. Ron is a writer.
   ____ c. Alan is sunburned.
                                    ____ f. Mopsy is fuzzy.

2. Fill in the following blanks using the names of the characters given above in exercise 1. Read carefully. Each group of sentences gives clues to help you choose.

   a. The patients waited for _____ at the hospital.

   b. Wherever _____ goes, people like him. He's always smiling and talking to everyone.

   c. _____ works at his typewriter. Sometimes his stories are in newspapers and magazines.

   d. I am cute and cuddly. Everyone likes to pet me. My name is _____ .

   e. _____ spends every Saturday in the sun.

   f. _____ laughs and asks us riddles.

Name _____

CREATE A CHARACTER

Make up a character. It could be a person, an animal, or a creature.

1. Tell about this character's personality. _____

_____

_____

2. Tell what the character looks like. _____

_____

3. What type of things does your character like to do? _____

_____

_____

4. Give your character a name and age.

_____

5. Where does your character live? Draw a picture of this character at home.

PLAN A TRIP

Pretend you are a travel agent. A character from a story you know has asked you to plan a vacation for him or her. Choose a character and make the plans!

1. Character's name: _____

2. Title and author: _____

   _____

3. Where would the character like to go? _____

4. Why would the character want to go there? _____

   _____

5. What type of transportation would you arrange for the trip?

   _____

6. Name six things the character would take on this trip.

   _____ _____ _____

   _____ _____ _____

7. Tell three things the character would do after arriving. _____

   _____

   _____

   _____

Beginning Book Reporting reproducible page, copyright © 1984 Pitman Learning, Inc.

PLAN A PARTY

Name one of your favorite story characters: _____

Name the book's title and author: _____

_____

Pretend you are planning a birthday party for this character.

1. Fill in an invitation!

    You are invited to a birthday party for:

    _____

    Date _____   Time _____

    Place _____

    Please RSVP to _____

2. Name two story characters you would invite.

    _____   _____

3. List three foods you would serve at the birthday party.

    _____ _____ _____

4. What gift would you buy for your character? _____

    Why did you choose this gift? _____

    _____

    _____

Name _____

FAVORITES

Who is your favorite character? _____

Title and author of story: _____

_____

The story may not tell you the character's favorite things, but you can guess them from the facts given in the story. Think about the character's personality and looks. Choose any four things from the list below. Write your character's favorites, and tell why you chose each one.

snack   vacation place   school subject
ice cream flavor   pet   book
outdoor game   indoor game   color

Example: Albert's favorite pet is his goldfish. Every day after
         school he goes home to watch the goldfish swim.

1. _____

_____

2. _____

_____

3. _____

_____

4. _____

_____

FACE TO FACE

Pretend you have a chance to talk to your favorite character. Write what you each might say. Two sentences have been started to give you some ideas. Finish them and add your own ideas.

_____ : Hello. I've wanted to meet you because
(Your name)
_____

_____ : _____
(Character's name)
_____

_____ : I'd like to talk to you about _____
(Your name)
_____

_____ : _____
(Character's name)
_____

_____ : _____
(Your name)
_____

_____ : _____
(Character's name)
_____

_____ : _____
(Your name)
_____

TEACHER'S NOTES

Your students will enjoy the activities in this unit throughout the year. The first three worksheets should be presented in order. Subsequent pages may be used in any order. Your creative thinkers will especially enjoy the last four activities. These worksheets may be used for brainstorming also. Remember the brainstorming rules: stick to the topic and accept everyone's suggestions.

IMPORTANT CHARACTERS
page 58

Objective: The student will identify heroes and heroines and their character qualities.

Suggestions for Use: Use this activity early in the year. The students will enjoy discussing their answers to Questions 1, 2, 3, 5, and 6.

Answer Key: 4. kind, brave, quick-thinking, honest, thoughtful, (beautiful, strong)

Discuss the fact that beauty and strength do not necessarily identify a hero or heroine. Have the students suggest other inner qualities they admire. Many TV shows portray heroines and heroes as having attractive appearances to enhance their admirable "inner" qualities. For this reason, many children will circle "beautiful" and "strong" in the list of hero or heroine qualities on Question 4. Discuss this predicament if your group is ready. A fairly sophisticated group of children will enjoy discussing how heroes and heroines are traditionally portrayed, especially in TV shows and movies. Let them talk about what "bad characters" look like too. Also, lead them to think of characters who break the image stereotypes.

MORE THAN SKIN DEEP
page 59

Objective: The student will complete a character description for a character of his or her choice and develop an awareness of how an author achieves characterization.

Suggestions for Use: Introduce this activity by making lists of physical characteristics and personality traits of characters the students know. Discuss how these "inside" and "outside" traits complement each other. This worksheet may be used as an independent activity for more capable students.

DESCRIBE A CHARACTER
page 60

Objective: The student will recognize characters by differentiating descriptions of looks and personalities.

Suggestions for Use: This worksheet can be completed independently.

Answer Key: 1a. P   b. P   c. L   d. L   e. P   f. L
2a. Dr. Hall   b. Ted   c. Ron   d. Mopsy   e. Alan   f. Sue

CREATE A CHARACTER
page 61

Objective: The student will apply knowledge of character descriptions to an imaginary character.

Suggestions for Use: Allow students to attempt this activity individually or cooperatively in small groups of three or four. Completion of the worksheet *Describe a Character* should precede *Create a Character*.

PLAN A TRIP
page 62

Objective: The student will demonstrate an understanding of characterization by planning an imaginary trip based on the character's traits.

Suggestions for Use: Use this page anytime you want a break from the usual discussion of character qualities. It is appropriate for independent work, and it is also a fun group activity. Encourage your students to consider the character's traits as they plan.

PLAN A PARTY
page 63

Objective: The student will demonstrate an understanding of a character's personality by planning a party for that character.

Suggestions for Use: This activity promotes divergent thinking. Encourage your students to use the personality traits established in the story while planning the party. Have the students share their responses.

FAVORITES
page 64

Objective: The student will demonstrate an understanding of characterization and apply the traits to a list of favorites.

Suggestions for Use: Many of these favorites will require creative or deductive thinking on the part of the student. Accept any response that is logical or sensible. Students writing about the same character may debate the "favorites" and the reasons for their choices. Also, it would be interesting to have the entire group analyze the same character independently and then to see how the choices match or diverge.

FACE TO FACE
page 65

Objective: The student will demonstrate an understanding of a character by writing an imaginary dialogue with this character.

Suggestions for Use: The students will enjoy reading their dialogues aloud. Accept any conversations reasonably consistent with the character's personality. You may wish to have the students complete the worksheet independently for the same character and then read their dialogues aloud for comparison.

UNIT FIVE

Seeing the Scene of the Story

Name _____

SETTING THE SCENE

In most stories, the author tells you where and when the story takes place. This is called setting the scene.

1. If you were an author, where would you put these characters? When might the story take place?

	Where	When
a. a princess	_____	_____
b. a cowboy	_____	_____
c. an astronaut	_____	_____
d. a pet pony	_____	_____
e. a talking dog	_____	_____
f. a curious girl	_____	_____
g. a football hero	_____	_____
h. a knight in armor	_____	_____

2. Make up two characters of your own. Name them and set the scenes for them.

	Name	Where	When
a.	_____	_____	_____
b.	_____	_____	_____

3. On the back, write a story about one of the characters.

Beginning Book Reporting reproducible page, copyright © 1984 Pitman Learning, Inc.

"SCENE" IN THE MIND

As you read, you imagine the scene of a story in your mind. Read the following story. Then complete the drawing of the scene in the box below.

The Scene

You can't miss Bojo Martin's large brick house. It sits in a grove of trees on a high hill just next to the "Welcome to Wellsley" sign. Every day at twelve noon, Bojo rings the huge yellow bell that hangs from his front porch. That's how everyone in Wellsley knows it's time for lunch. Today when twelve noon came, no bell sound filled the air. The bell was gone!

USING THE MIND'S EYE

An author wants you to imagine the scene of a story in your mind. Draw what you see in "your mind's eye" as you read each of these scenes.

Scene 1: The night was dark. Jane heard an owl hooting in the tree in the backyard. The trashcans looked like monsters.

Draw scene 2 on the back of this page.

Scene 2: Jack decided to explore his new neighborhood. The big, brick houses seemed very new. He wondered if any children lived nearby. Then he noticed two bicycles leaning on the fence at the house next door.

A FAIRY TALE SETTING

1. Answer these questions.

   a. What is your favorite fairy tale? _____

   b. Who is the main character? _____

   c. Where does this fairy tale take place? _____

2. Now imagine you can wave a magic wand and move this fairy tale into today's world! What would be different?

   a. What clothes would the main character wear? _____

   _____

   b. What new things would the main character have to learn how to do? _____

   _____

   _____

   c. Would the character's problem be different? _____

   How could the problem be solved today? _____

   _____

   _____

   d. How could you help this character get along in the new setting? _____

   _____

CHANGING THE SETTING

On another piece of paper, write the facts for a story you read.
- title
- author
- characters
- setting—place
- setting—time
- exciting events

Now change the setting—the place and the time. Tell how this would change the story. Complete the following.

1. The new setting is _____

2. The characters would have to learn how to _____

_____

3. Tell how the main problem of the story would change in this setting. _____

_____

4. Name two things that would surprise the characters in this new setting. _____

_____

5. What would the characters do for fun in this new setting?

_____

6. Tell two other things that might be different in this new setting. _____

_____

Beginning Book Reporting reproducible page, copyright © 1984 Pitman Learning, Inc.

TEACHER'S NOTES

Appreciating and visualizing the scene of a story will add to the reader's enjoyment. The activities in this unit are designed to enhance the appreciation of the setting for the student reader. Authorities agree that television has become reality for many viewers; understanding that setting is purely the whim of the author may strengthen your students' awareness of the nonreality of many television programs.

SETTING THE SCENE
page 70

Objective: The student will choose appropriate settings for the given characters.

Suggestions for Use: Use this as an individual activity. Accept any answers that are logical. The students will enjoy sharing their ideas. The invented characters should lead the children to write some interesting stories. Often, a distinctive character and a well-defined setting will suggest a plot for further development.

"SCENE" IN THE MIND
page 71

Objective: The student will interpret written descriptions of setting by completing a drawing of a setting.

Suggestions for Use: Cut out large, simple pictures from magazines or other sources. Describe each picture verbally to the students without letting them see it. Ask the students to try to imagine what the pictures look like. Then show them the pictures and ask how many students pictured similar scenes.

Distribute an activity worksheet to each student. Explain that the reader should try to imagine the scene the author is creating. Allow them to read the worksheet silently, aloud, or both. Then direct the students to complete the drawing based on the scene they have read. Post completed drawings after the results have been shared with the class.

USING THE MIND'S EYE
page 72

Objective: The student will interpret written descriptions of setting.

Suggestions for Use: Visualizing a setting from the author's clues is a key to story enjoyment and appreciation. Introduce your students to the term "the mind's eye" and have them practice using "the mind's eye" often! When you read aloud, you can pause after a key description and have them verbalize them or draw their mental images. Tape-record stories that contain directions to stop the tape and draw what the listener sees. Have the stories available at a listening center.

A FAIRY TALE SETTING
page 73

Objective: The student will demonstrate an understanding of the relationship between setting and plot by making appropriate changes for a fairy tale of her or his choice.

Suggestions for Use: Use this activity after the students have enjoyed a fairy tale. Accept any responses that fit. Reverse this activity by having the students change a "real" setting to an imaginary setting. Use a story with a realistic setting. Ask the students to replace the setting with a land of magic and fantasy and then to tell how the story's plot would change.

CHANGING THE SETTING
page 74

Objective: The student will demonstrate an understanding of the relationship between plot and setting.

Suggestions for Use: Use this activity after your students have successfully completed the preceding one. The students may enjoy illustrating their characters in the new settings.

UNIT SIX

Something for Everyone

FANTASY FICTION

Some stories seem as if they could not really happen. These stories may be called fantasy. Fill in some facts for a fantasy that you have read.

1. Title: _____

2. Author: _____

3. Are all the characters people? _____

4. Are all speaking characters people? _____

5. What is the setting of this story?

    place: _____

    time: _____

6. What happened in the story that could not happen in real

    life? _____

_____

7. Why do you think this story is a fantasy? _____

_____

_____

_____

REALISTIC FICTION

Some stories seem very real. You might think they really happened. Stories that seem as if they could happen are called realistic fiction. Fill in some facts for a realistic story that you have read.

1. Title: _____

2. Author: _____

3. Are all the characters people? _____

4. Are all speaking characters people? _____

5. What is the setting of this story?

   place: _____

   time: _____

6. Name two important things that happened in this story

   which could happen in real life. _____

   _____

   _____

   _____

DON'T PUT ALL YOUR BOOKS IN ONE BASKET

Authors write books about many subjects. Read the book descriptions in Column I and place their letters in the matching subject baskets in Column II.

Column I   Column II

a. George Washington, the first president of the United States, lived at Mt. Vernon.

b. The three little pigs built houses to save themselves from the wolf.

c. Fair Wind, a horse of great speed and beauty, won every race. Now he is lame.

d. No one had ever won the race in less than ten minutes. Jan wanted to set a new record.

e. The safe showed no signs of forced entry, but the money was gone. Who took it, and how?

Which subject basket most interests you? _____

Name _____

WHAT IS A BIOGRAPHY?

A biography is a book about the life of a real person. If a person writes a book about himself or herself, it is called an autobiography. When you read a biography, you learn about the main events in the person's life. You find out what makes that person special. If the person is no longer living, you may also find out why we remember that person.

Fill in some facts for a biography or autobiography you have read.

1. Title: _____

2. Author: _____

3. Who is the real person? _____

4. Tell two main events in this person's life.

    a. _____

    b. _____

5. What was special about this person? _____

_____

_____

6. What did you like or dislike about this biography? _____

_____

_____

ENJOYING NONFICTION

One reason to read nonfiction books is to get more information about a subject.

1. What subject would you like to know more about? _____

_____

2. List three questions you have about this subject.

   a. _____

   b. _____

   c. _____

Find some books on this subject at the library. Use the card catalog or ask the librarian. Choose a book you think may answer your questions about the subject you are interested in. After reading the book, fill in these blanks.

3. Title and author: _____

_____

4. Did the book answer the three questions you had about this

   subject? _____

5. Do you have any new questions about this subject? _____
   If so, explain on the back of this page.

Beginning Book Reporting reproducible page, copyright © 1984 Pitman Learning, Inc.

NONFICTION BOOK
REPORT FORM

Answer these questions about a nonfiction book you have read.

1. What is the title? _____

2. Who is the author? _____

3. What is the subject or main idea? _____

_____

4. What new facts did you learn? Tell three.

    a. _____

    b. _____

    c. _____

5. Give your opinion of the book, and tell why you did or did

    not enjoy it. Give examples in your answer! _____

_____

_____

_____

_____

EXTRA! EXTRA! READ ALL ABOUT IT!

I just read an incredible book! The title of the

book is _____ , and the

author is _____ . You can

find this book in the _____
                        (fiction or nonfiction?)

section of the library.

Let me tell you a few things about this book.

_____

_____

_____

_____

_____

_____

_____

Name _____

ENJOYING POETRY

Find a poem you have enjoyed.

Title of poem _____

Poet (author) _____

Copy your poem here.

_____

_____

_____

_____

_____

_____

_____

_____

_____

_____

Tell why you liked this poem. _____

_____

_____

Name _____

POETRY IS FOR SPECIAL FEELINGS

A poet may write a poem to make you feel the same way that he or she feels. Find a poem that makes you feel something special. Think about how the poet might have felt, too.

1. Answer these questions about the poem you have read.

   a. What is the poem's title? _____

   b. Who is the poet (author)? _____

   c. What is the subject or main idea in this poem? _____

   _____

   _____

   d. How did you feel when you read this poem? _____

   _____

   _____

   e. List some words or phrases from the poem that made you feel this way.

   _____   _____

   _____   _____

On the back of this page, make a drawing about this poem.

Beginning Book Reporting reproducible page, copyright © 1984 Pitman Learning, Inc.

Name _____

RHYMING POETRY

Some poems have words that rhyme. This means that the word endings sound alike. Rhyming words are fun to read aloud. They help make it easier to remember the poem too.

Find a poem that has rhyming words.

1. What is the title? _____

2. Who is the poet (author)? _____

3. What is the main idea in this poem? _____

_____

_____

_____

4. List some rhyming words from this poem.

_____ _____ _____

_____ _____ _____

5. Write your favorite line from this poem. _____

_____

_____

TEACHER'S NOTES

There really is something for everyone! There are books to suit every taste. In fact, many students are dissatisfied with a constant diet of fiction. Some students prefer reading nonfiction. Some students enjoy reading poetry. Use some of the activities in this unit to satisfy their literary appetites.

Introduce your students to the nonfiction section of the library. They may not be ready to master the Dewey decimal system, but knowledge of the sections that are of interest to their age group will encourage them to read more. Have them locate books that correlate with your current social studies or science units as well as with their personal interests. If you do not have a school library, plan a field trip to the neighborhood library, or check out books for them.

FANTASY FICTION And REALISTIC FICTION
pages 78–79

Objective: The student will list characteristics of a story reflecting fantasy and a story composed of realistic fiction.

Suggestions for Use: Use these worksheets as independent activities. Conduct a follow-up discussion for each worksheet. Have the students name their favorite fairy tales, folktales, and other stories or books that contain fantasy. Give examples of realistic fiction to contrast the students' examples of fantasy. This will help clarify the difference between realistic and fantasy fiction. Avoid using the word "imaginary" to explain "fantasy." Since an author determines all elements of a story, both types of fiction will be "imagined." Also, avoid confusing the distinction between realistic and fantasy fiction with the nonfiction/fiction distinction.

DON'T PUT ALL YOUR BOOKS IN ONE BASKET
page 80

Objective: The student will recognize that books are written about a variety of subjects and can be categorized.

Suggestions for Use: From your school library, gather two books exemplifying each of the categories shown (animal story, adventure, famous person, mystery, and fairy tale). Tell a little about each book. Then, ask the students to pair the books according to subject. Write the paired titles on the board and give the appropriate category titles for each pair.

Have the students read and complete the worksheet, either individually or together as a class activity. Discuss their answers. When the students visit the school library, have them bring their worksheets.

Introduce additional categories, and encourage them to select books from the categories that most interest them.

Answer Key: 1. e; 2. d; 3. a; 4. c; 5. b

WHAT IS A BIOGRAPHY?
page 81

Objective: The student will write a report about a biography or auto-biography he or she has enjoyed.

Suggestions for Use: Throughout the school year, your students will enjoy reading about famous people. Capitalize on their natural interest in real-life heroes and heroines by introducing them to biographies. This worksheet assumes the student has some familiarity with the book reporting strategy for fiction. If you wish, the students may write their book report information in complete sentences or in paragraphs. You may wish to make a display of the reports your group has prepared to encourage other students to read biographies.

ENJOYING NONFICTION
page 82

Objective: The student will choose a nonfiction book to read and use as a resource.

Suggestions for Use: Help your students determine topics that interest them. This worksheet could designate a beginning research activity as well as a book reporting activity. Encourage self-sufficiency and the use of card catalogs and other library tools. Students will enjoy sharing the information they discover.

NONFICTION BOOK REPORT FORM
page 83

Objective: The student will report on a nonfiction book read independently.

Suggestions for Use: Distribute this worksheet any time to students wishing to report on a nonfiction book. This activity assumes the student has some familiarity with the book reporting strategy for fiction. You may wish to give a badge to each student who completes this assignment. To expand the activity, have the student write the report in paragraph form. Paragraph 1 should include the title, author, main idea, and new facts. Paragraph 2 should offer opinions (with reasons) about the book.

Introduce your students to the term "bibliography." Direct them to look in the back of their nonfiction books to locate the bibliography. Have the students try to find a couple of the books listed in the bibliography by checking the card catalog or asking the librarian.

EXTRA! EXTRA! READ ALL ABOUT IT!
page 84

Objective: The student will write general information about any book read independently.

Suggestions for Use: Use this worksheet as a general book reporting form to motivate students to provide detail or to express enthusiasm about the books they've read. This worksheet gives students an opportunity to be less formal in their book reporting. You may wish to make a bulletin board display or compile an "archive" of these informal reports. Treat them as if they are special news reports.

ENJOYING POETRY
page 85

Objective: The student will read and copy a poem of her or his own choosing.

Suggestions for Use: Most poetry is meant to be heard. Read poetry aloud to your students as often as you can. Encourage your students to memorize short poems. Have the group practice choral reading, and prepare choral readings to give to other groups. Your students may enjoy illustrating a poem after you read the poem aloud. Display their illustrations on a bulletin board beside a copy of the poem.

POETRY IS FOR SPECIAL FEELINGS
page 86

Objective: The student will apply the basic book reporting strategy to poetry that expresses emotions.

Suggestions for Use: Use this worksheet for an independent activity. Precede the activity with a discussion of how poetry might express special feelings. Choose a poem to read aloud. Tell the main idea to the group and describe how it makes you feel. Then ask the students to tell how they feel. Isolate certain words and phrases in the poem that express emotions.

RHYMING POETRY
page 87

Objective: The student will apply the basic book reporting strategy to rhyming poetry.

Suggestions for Use: Use this worksheet for an independent activity. However, the poems that the students choose are probably meant to be read aloud, so let the students share their poems with each other. Encourage the students to memorize their poems.

UNIT SEVEN

Get Your Group Reading More

Name _____

BE A BOOKWORM

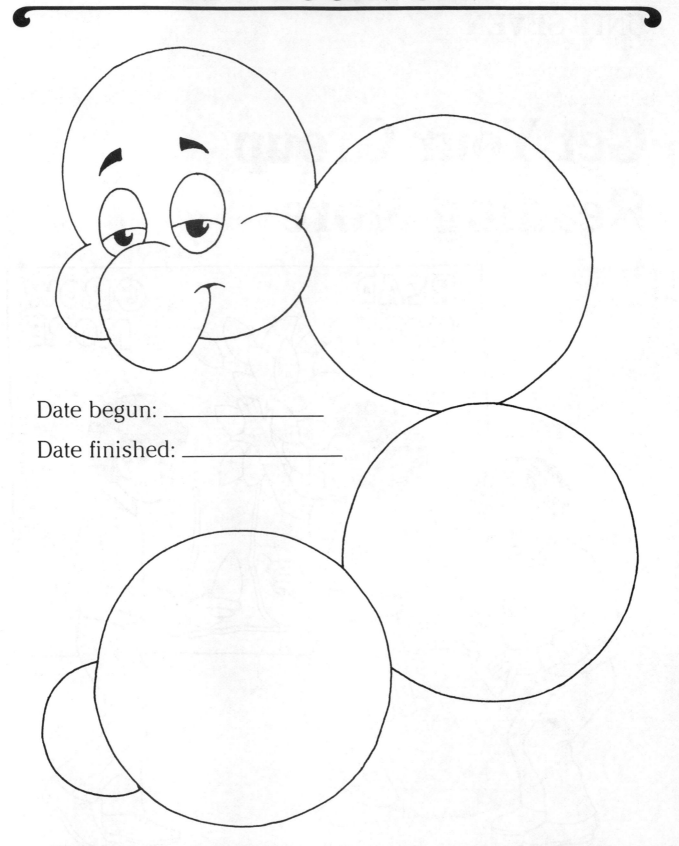

Date begun: _____

Date finished: _____

BOOKWORM SEGMENTS

Fill out a bookworm segment for each book you have read. Write the title and author of the book. Then write about one exciting event. Cut out the segments and paste them on the bookworm.

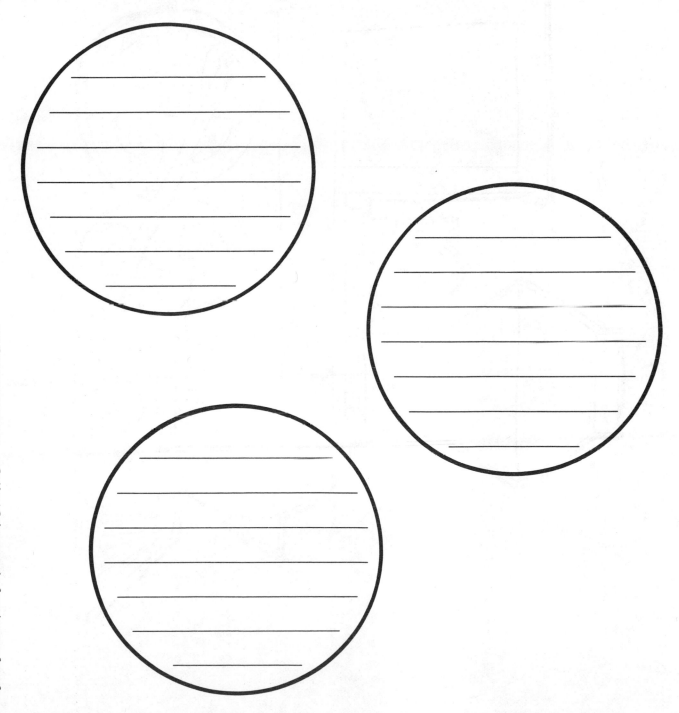

BOOK TRAIN ENGINE

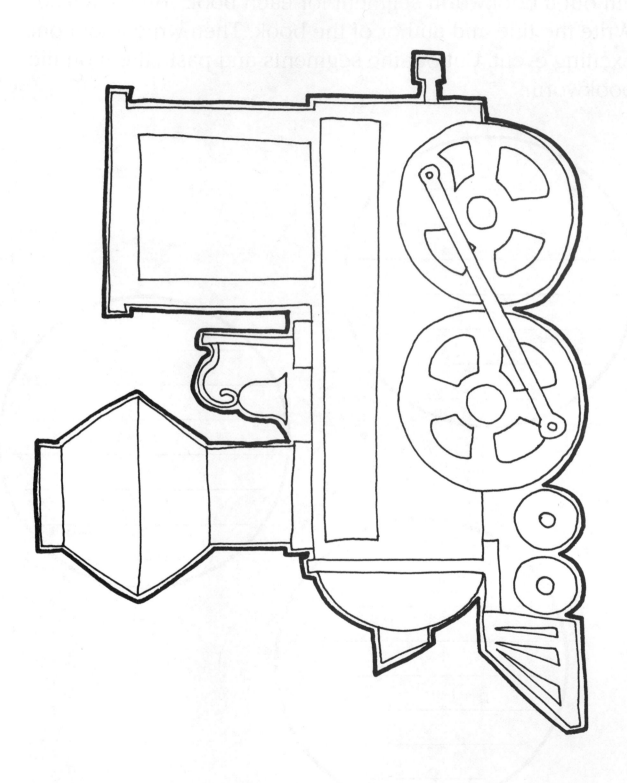

BOOK TRAIN CAR

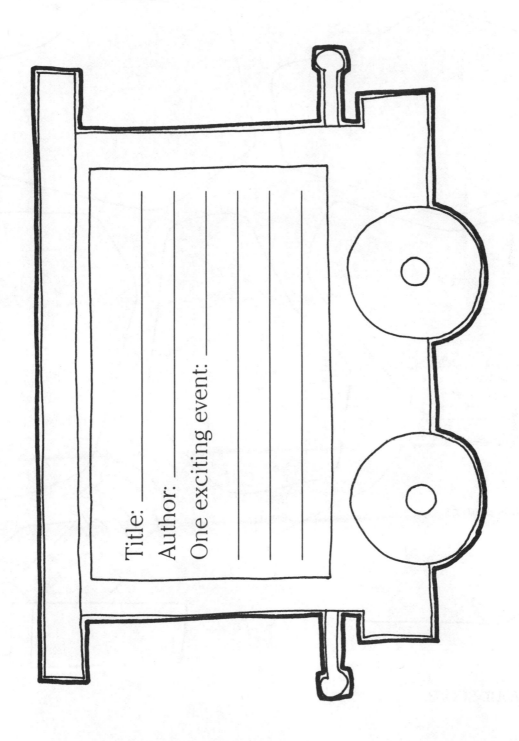

Title: _____

Author: _____

One exciting event: _____

BLASTING ASTEROIDS

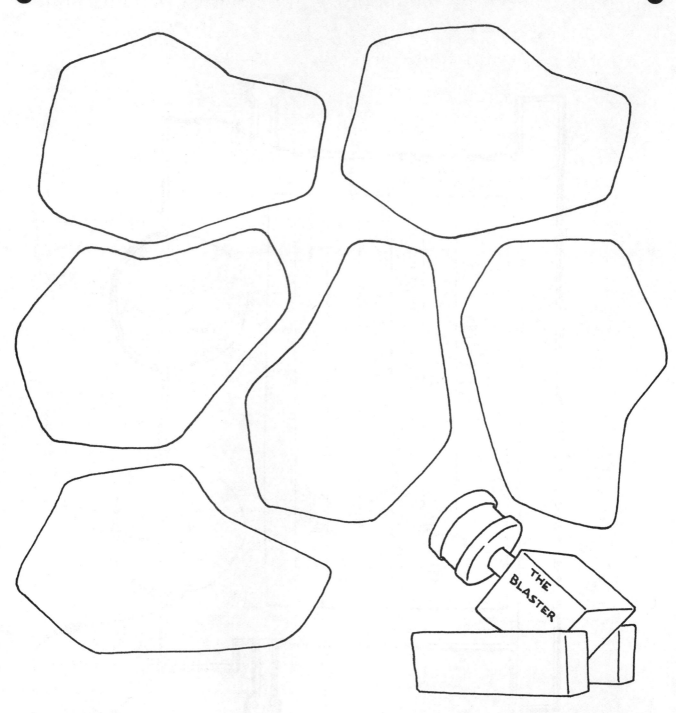

Keep your score.

Book $\frac{\quad}{\#1}$ + $\frac{\quad}{\#2}$ + $\frac{\quad}{\#3}$ + $\frac{\quad}{\#4}$ + $\frac{\quad}{\#5}$ + $\frac{\quad}{\#6}$ = $\frac{\quad}{\text{TOTAL}}$

ASTEROIDS

Fill in an asteroid for each book you have read. Write the title and author. Paste the asteroids in place on the *Blasting Asteroids* page and keep score!

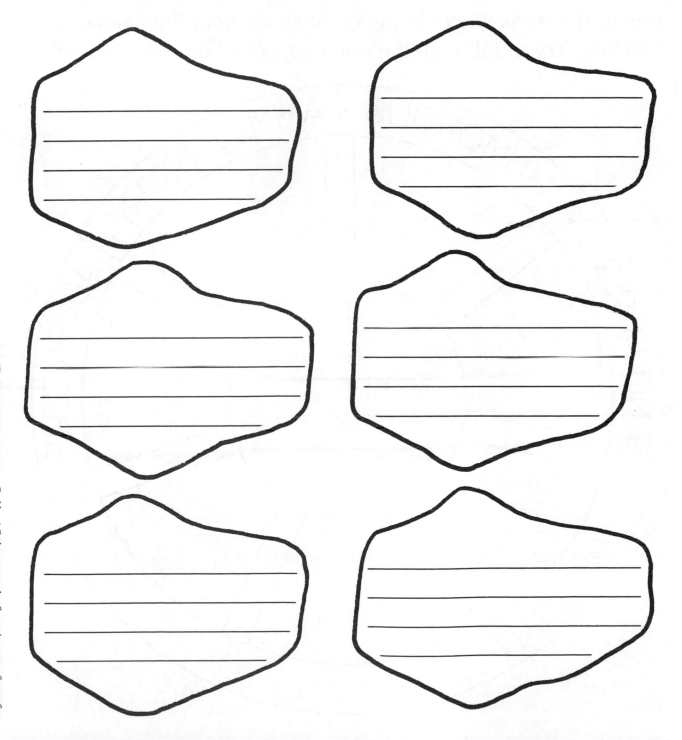

BOOK WHEEL

The book wheel shows five possible categories of books and two more categories for you to choose. When you have read a book from one of the categories on the book wheel, write the title in the book wheel in the open space near the category heading. Try to fill in all the open spaces of the book wheel!

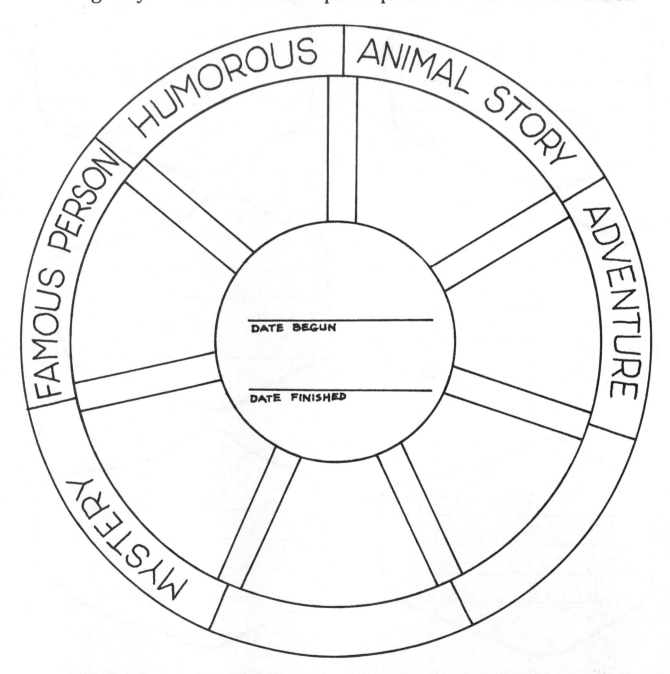

HUMOROUS

ANIMAL STORY

FAMOUS PERSON

ADVENTURE

DATE BEGUN _____

DATE FINISHED _____

MYSTERY

Name _____

CATEGORIES

	Animal	Humorous	Famous Person	Nonfiction
Title				
Author				
Why I liked this book:				

"RACE TRACK READERS" RACE TRACK

START

FINISH

Beginning Book Reporting reproducible page, copyright © 1984 Pitman Learning, Inc.

"RACE TRACK READERS"
RACE CARS

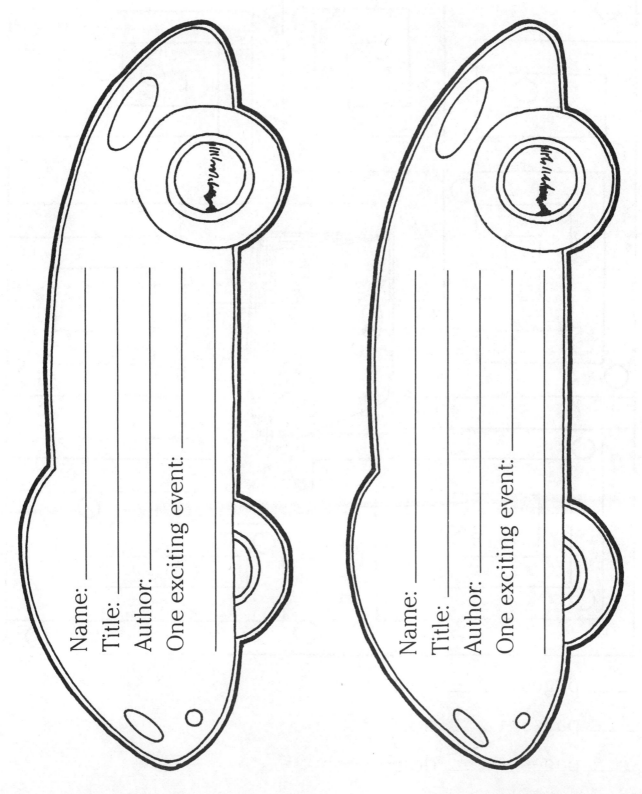

Name: _____
Title: _____
Author: _____
One exciting event: _____

Name: _____
Title: _____
Author: _____
One exciting event: _____

BOOKMAN

_____ pages = _____ dots

_____ pages = _____ dots

_____ pages = _____ dots

Beginning Book Reporting reproducible page, copyright © 1984 Pitman Learning, Inc.

BOOK TREES—LEAVES

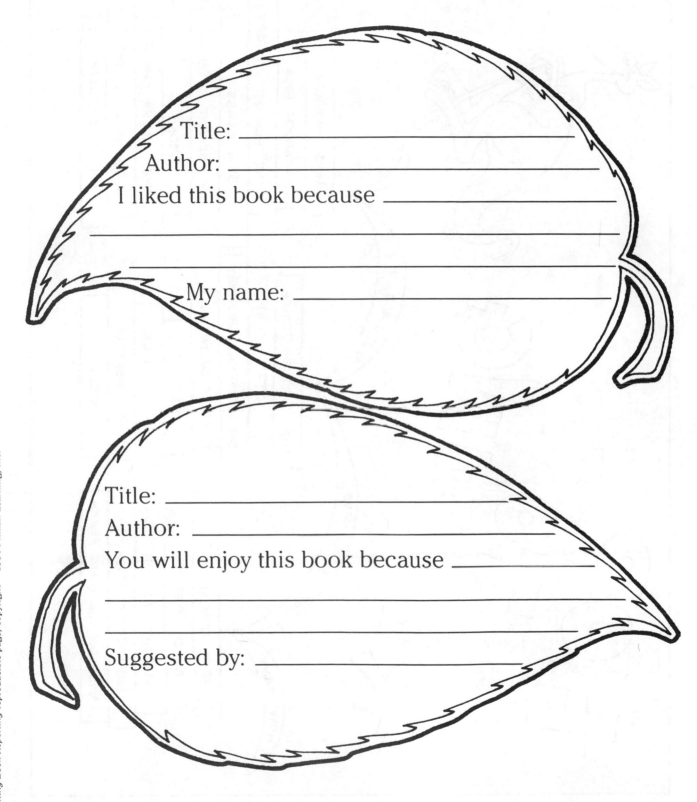

Title: _____

Author: _____

I liked this book because _____

_____

_____

My name: _____

Title: _____

Author: _____

You will enjoy this book because _____

_____

_____

Suggested by: _____

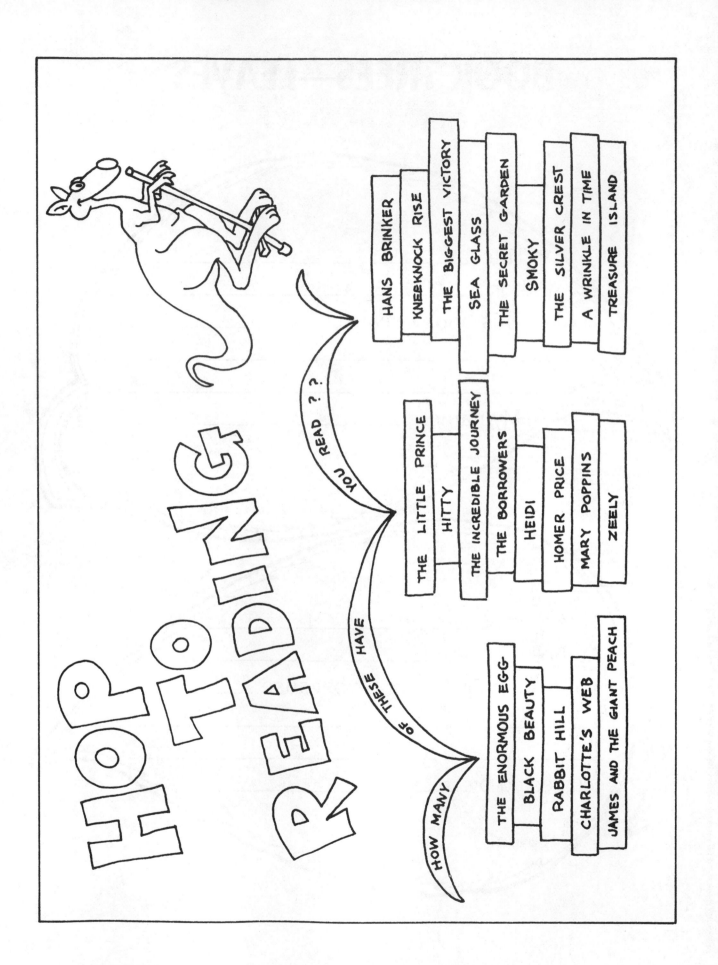

HOP TO READING

HOW MANY OF THESE HAVE YOU READ ??

HANS BRINKER
KNEEKNOCK RISE
THE BIGGEST VICTORY
SEA GLASS
THE SECRET GARDEN
SMOKY
THE SILVER CREST
A WRINKLE IN TIME
TREASURE ISLAND

THE LITTLE PRINCE
HITTY
THE INCREDIBLE JOURNEY
THE BORROWERS
HEIDI
HOMER PRICE
MARY POPPINS
ZEELY

THE ENORMOUS EGG
BLACK BEAUTY
RABBIT HILL
CHARLOTTE'S WEB
JAMES AND THE GIANT PEACH

"HOP TO READING"
KANGAROO

"JOIN THE BOOK CREW" BOAT

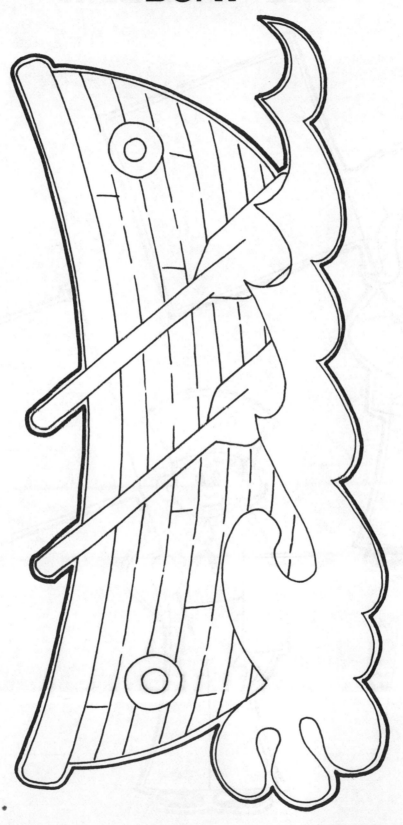

"JOIN THE BOOK CREW"
CREW MEMBERS

GUIDE TO GREAT READING

Title: _____

Author: _____

Contributed by: _____
        (Your name)

Write two or more sentences about this book. Tell something
that will make a friend want to read this book.

_____

_____

_____

Draw an interesting scene from this book.

TRADE-A-BOOK PARENT INFORMATION LETTER

Dear Parent,

To stimulate interest in books and reading, _____ (class, school) is planning a Trade-a-Book Day. We (I) hope you will give us your support by giving your child permission to bring in children's books to trade. Each book brought in will entitle your child to a book in trade on Trade-a-Book Day. Receipts will be issued for the books received from your child. The receipts should be retained, and they will be used to trade for other books on Trade-a-Book Day.

Books to be traded should be in good condition, and your child must agree to part with the books. The books for trade should be turned in by _____ (date) . The books should be brought to _____ (location) . Trade-a-Book Day will be held on _____ (date) from _____ (time) to _____ (time) in _____ (location) .

Your cooperation and encouragement will ensure a successful Trade-a-Book Day. We (I) thank you in advance.

Sincerely,

Beginning Book Reporting reproducible page, copyright © 1984 Pitman Learning, Inc.

TRADE-A-BOOK
PERMISSION SLIP

I give my child, _____ , permission to trade the
(Name)

following book(s) on Trade-a-Book Day. (Please list the titles
below.)

_____   _____
(Date)   (Signature)

This certificate entitles _____ to receive _____
(Name)   (No. of titles
                                                                                                    listed above)

book(s) on Trade-a-Book Day.

_____
(Signature)

BADGES FOR READERS

HAPPY

I READ ___ BOOKS

Book Worm Books

Tooting My Horn!!

TTT

___ Books

I'm wise!
I read
___ Books

CERTIFICATES

Beautiful Reading

_____

_____

_____

READING STAR

_____

_____

_____

BOOKMARKERS

DOOR TO
GOOD
READING

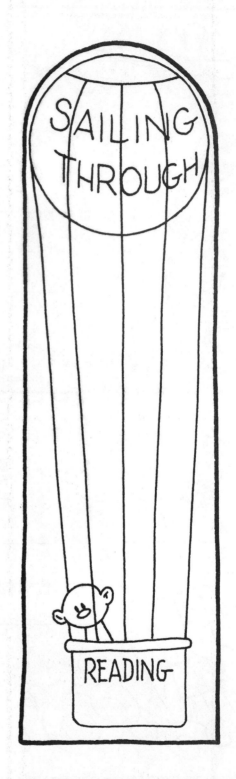

SAILING
THROUGH

READING

BOOKMARKERS

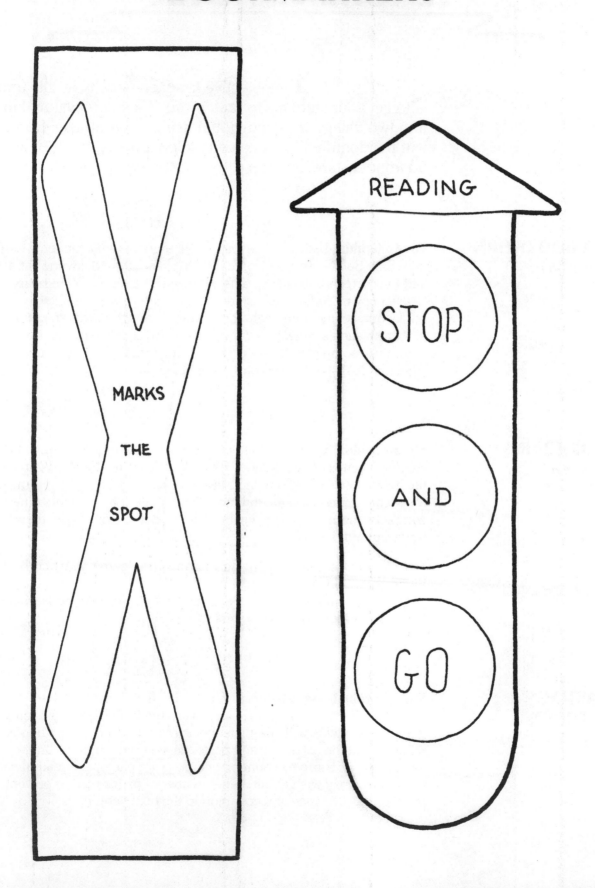

MARKS THE SPOT

READING

STOP

AND

GO

TEACHER'S NOTES

The objective for each activity in this unit is to get your students to read more! These motivators fall into two categories—individual use and group use. Each will be identified to make your selection easier. All bulletin board ideas are, or course, for group use.

BE A BOOKWORM
pages 92-93

For Individual Use: This motivator will encourage the students to read until their bookworms are complete. Duplicate the bookworm form and the corresponding segments on unlined white or colored paper. Give a copy of both to each student. The student will complete a bookworm segment for each book read. He or she may then cut out and paste each segment on the bookworm form. Have the students color their completed bookworms. Display them around the room, on students' desks, or in any convenient place.

BOOK TRAIN
pages 94-95

For Individual Use: Duplicate an engine and several cars for each student. Each student should write his or her name in the box above the train wheels on the engine. Have the students fill in the information for each book read on the train car. Each student may connect the completed train cars to the engine. The students can display their book trains around their desks.

For Group Use: Make an engine with the class name on it and post it in the classroom. Give each student a train car for each book read. Attach the student train cars to the class engine to make a book train that goes all the way around the room!

BLASTING ASTEROIDS
pages 96-97

For Individual Use: Challenge your students to blast the asteroids by reading good books. Duplicate and distribute both pages for each student. The students will complete the asteroid blasters for six books read, cut out the asteroids, and paste the asteroids in place on the asteroid form. Score by counting one point for each <u>page</u> read of each book. (You may wish to initial the number of pages read to prevent problems.) Give special recognition to the high scorers!

BOOK WHEEL
page 98

For Individual Use: The *Book Wheel* is a long-range reading record that will encourage your students to read different types of books. Duplicate one book wheel for each student. Give reading certificates or badges to students who complete their book wheels within a given time period.

CATEGORIES
page 99

For Individual Use: *Categories*, like *Book Wheel*, will encourage your students to read a variety of books. You may wish to adapt the categories to the interests of your students before duplicating the page. Provide one sheet for each student. Give a reading certificate or badge to students completing their charts within a given time period.

"RACE TRACK READERS" BULLETIN BOARD
pages 100–101

Help children to join the reading race!

Materials
- transparency of the race track linemaster
- paper for bulletin board background
- construction paper for caption letters
- several copies of race track cars—one car for each book read by a student. (Duplicate the race car linemaster on colored construction paper.)
- markers
- stapler
- scissors

Procedure
1. Staple the background paper to the bulletin board.
2. Project the race track transparency onto the background paper with an overhead projector. Arrange the projection size to fit your board. Outline the image projected on the background paper.
3. Cut letters for the caption and staple them to the board.
4. Cut out the race cars. Distribute a few to each student.
5. Have the students design their racing cars with distinctive markings.
6. Each space on the track represents one book read. Students begin at the starting line, placing one car for each book completed in consecutive spaces until the finish line is reached.

Variation
Label each section of the course with a book category—for example, biography, fairy tale, folktale, animal story, adventure story, "how-to" selection, and mystery story. Students will fill out their race cars for books read and staple them in the proper category spaces on the track.

BOOKMAN
page 102

For Individual Use: Encourage your students to read their way through the Bookman corridors. Duplicate one Bookman maze for each student. Decide how many dots can be "gobbled up" in relation to the length of the book: the longer the book, the more dots that can be gobbled up. For example, a book of 10–30 pages earns one dot, a book of 31–50 pages earns two dots, and a book of more than 50 pages earns three dots. The reader will color dots to signify that the dots have been "eaten." Have the students use a different color for each book. When all the dots have been gobbled up (colored), the students may hand in their Bookman mazes for display. (Note that there is no route or destination for the Bookman. The "gobbling" is random.)

"BOOK TREES" BULLETIN BOARD
page 103

Set aside a bulletin board for the Book Tree. Place background paper on the bulletin board if you wish. Make an outline of a tree trunk with branches, using brown yarn. Staple or pin it to the bulletin board. Duplicate the leaves on colored construction paper. (As the seasons change, alter the color you use.) When a student finishes reading a book, he or she may fill out a leaf and put it on the tree.

"HOP TO READING" BULLETIN BOARD
pages 104–105

Materials
- enlargement of the kangaroo (Use the transparency projection method—see teacher's notes for *Race Track Readers.*)
- bulletin board background paper
- curved strips made from construction paper (to designate the kangaroo's path)
- construction paper rectangles of various sizes
- construction paper for caption letters
- felt-tipped markers
- scissors
- stapler

Procedure
1. Staple the background paper to the bulletin board.
2. Cut out the caption letters and staple them to the board.
3. Print the challenge question "How many of these have you read?" on the curved strips as shown. Staple them to the board.

4. Print book titles on the construction paper rectangles. You may wish to design these rectangles to look like book spines. Stack the rectangles to resemble books. Staple the stacks under each "bounce" point as shown. (The number of book titles you use is at your discretion, as are the titles you select. Try to select books that are readily available from your school library.)
5. Staple the kangaroo enlargement to the board as shown. (The size you make the kangaroo will depend on the board space you have available.)

Variation
Have the students print (on the rectangles) titles of books they have read and enjoyed. The students might also write their names on the rectangles.

"JOIN THE BOOK CREW" BULLETIN BOARD
pages 106–108

Materials
● enlargements of the boat (Use the transparency projection method described in the teacher's notes for *Race Track Readers*.)
● copies of the crew members (one for each student)
● bulletin board background paper
● construction paper for caption letters
● felt-tipped markers
● scissors
● stapler

Procedure
1. Staple the background paper to the bulletin board.
2. Cut out the caption and staple it to the board.
3. Cut out as many boat enlargements as you need for the class. Staple them to the board, leaving tops of boats open.
4. Give a crew member to each student in your class. Have the students color and cut out the figures and print their names on the hats.
5. Students will write each book title on their crew members' flags after reading a book.
6. Staple the completed figures to the board, tucked in the boats.

GUIDE TO GREAT READING
page 109

For Group Use: Have your students make a Book Guide for their classroom or school library. When a student finishes reading a book, he or she may complete a Book Guide sheet. When ten or more sheets have accumulated, make a Book Guide volume, using tagboard for a cover and brads to hold the book together. Encourage your students to refer to the Book Guide when they are looking for new books to read. If you wish, award badges to Book Guide contributors. Keep the Book Guides from previous years as motivators. Get the whole school involved: encourage each class to prepare a Book Guide. Store them in the library.

TRADE-A-BOOK
pages 110–111

For Group Use (all school): Have students bring in books that their families no longer want. Each book earns a book trading ticket to be redeemed on Trade-a-Book Day. Get the approval of your administration for this project, especially if you plan to involve more than one class. Write a letter about Trade-a-Book or adapt the parent information letter on page 110 to suit your needs. Plan an advertising campaign with your group to spark interest. Prepare and distribute the parent information letters and permission slips. Include the book turn-in dates, the date for the Trade-a-Book Day, and your objective. Have an adult supervise the book collections. Check the books for suitability and overall condition. Have your students sort the books by categories. Bring extra books in case some children want to collect books but are unable to bring any for trading. If other classes are involved, make a schedule for their visits. Leftover books may be donated to a local charity. Get the P.T.A. involved by suggesting they conduct a book swap for adults!

BADGES FOR READERS
page 112

For Individual Use: Color and laminate the badges before cutting them out. Attach a tape loop to the back of the badge so the student can easily wear the badge. Award badges to students who have completed reading goals.

CERTIFICATES
page 113

For Individual Use: Award a certificate to anyone who meets a reading goal. The students may color the certificate with crayons or felt-tipped markers.

BOOKMARKERS
pages 114–115

For Individual Use: Duplicate the bookmarkers on colored construction paper or on unlined white paper if you want the students to color them. Cut out the markers and give them to students as prizes for good reading work.

For Group Use: Make enlargements of the bookmarkers with an overhead projector. Post the enlarged bookmarkers around the classroom. Allow the students to color them.